PETER L. BERGER

RELIGION IN A
REVOLUTIONARY SOCIETY

Distinguished Lecture Series
on
the Bicentennial

This lecture is one in a series sponsored
by the American Enterprise Institute
in celebration of the Bicentennial of the United States.
The views expressed are those of the lecturers
and do not necessarily reflect
the views of the staff, officers or trustees of AEI.
All of the lectures in this series will be
collected later in a single volume.

revolution · continuity · promise

PETER L. BERGER

RELIGION IN A REVOLUTIONARY SOCIETY

Delivered at
Christ Church, Alexandria, Virginia
on February 4, 1974

American Enterprise Institute for Public Policy Research
Washington, D. C.

© 1974 by American Enterprise Institute
for Public Policy Research, Washington, D.C.

ISBN 0-8447-1306-6

Library of Congress Catalog Card Number L.C. 74-79895

Printed in the United States of America

The title of this address, as it was given to me, implies a formidable assignment—no less than the overall consideration of the place of religion in contemporary America. I have some reservations about applying the adjective "revolutionary" to American society. But, minimally, it refers to something very real in that society—namely, its quality of rapid and far-reaching change—and for this reason I describe our present society, not just that of 1776, as revolutionary.

This quality of change makes my assignment all the more difficult. It is a source of constant embarrassment to all commentators and forecasters. Just look what happened to the most celebrated diagnoses of our situation during the last decade: Harvey Cox published his best-selling beatification of the new urbanism just before everyone agreed that American cities had become unfit for civilized habitation. The proclamation of the death of God hit the cover of *Time* magazine just before the onset of a massive resurgence of flamboyant supernaturalism. More recently, those who were betting on the greening of America led the Democratic party to one of its biggest electoral defeats in history. And just now, when Daniel Bell has impressively proclaimed the coming of post-industrial society, the energy crisis makes one think that we will be lucky if we manage to stay around as an *industrial* society. Perhaps the only advice one can give to the sociological prophet is to write his book quickly, and then go into hiding—or, alternatively, to be very, very careful. This is not a book, but I intend to be careful. This means, among other things, that I cannot

1

spare you some pedantic distinctions, qualifications, and less-than-inspiring formulations.

I

The consideration before me involves some sort of answer to the question "where are we at?" To try for this answer, it will help to find a date in the past with which to compare the present moment. If one wants to make rather sweeping statements, one will likely pick a date far back in history, like 1776, or the time of the Reformation, or even the late Ice Age (as Andrew Greeley did recently—his thesis being that "the basic human religious needs and the basic religious functions have not changed very notably since the late Ice Age," the credibility of which thesis clearly hinges on one's understanding of "basic"). Taking seriously my own warning to be careful, I propose to take a much more recent date: 1955. This happens to be the year in which an important book on American religion was published, Will Herberg's *Protestant–Catholic–Jew*.[1] More important, though, the mid-1950s were the years just before a number of significant ruptures in the course of American religion and of American society generally (ruptures, incidentally, which no one foresaw). It is a convenient date with which to compare the present moment. In attempting to meet my assignment, therefore, I will concentrate on two questions: *What was the situation of American religion about 1955? What has happened to it since then?*

Since this period has of late become the subject of intensive nostalgia, I should add that my choice of date is non-nostalgically motivated. I was wonderfully young at the time, and I am all too susceptible to reminiscing about my youth in a rosy glow of memories. I am quite sure that I and my contemporaries had no notion *then* of living in a particularly rosy time. It is probably inevitable that we look back on the time of our youth as some sort of Golden Age. I imagine that this was the case with individuals

---

[1] Will Herberg, *Protestant–Catholic–Jew: An Essay in American Religious Sociology* (Garden City, N.Y.: Doubleday & Co., Inc., 1955).

2

who were young during the Black Death or the invasions of Genghis Khan. There is a temptation to project one's own decline since then to the society at large. The temptation is to be resisted.

In other words, the comparison between 1955 and 1974 is not necessarily odious. But before I start comparing, I must elaborate one very essential distinction, the distinction between *denominational religion* and *civil religion*.

Denominational religion in America refers to what most people mean when they speak of religion—the bodies of Christian and Jewish tradition as these are enshrined in the major religious organizations in this country. Denominational religion is the religion of the churches. The plural, *churches,* is very important: there are many churches in America, and for a long time now they have existed side by side under conditions of legal equality. Indeed, Richard Niebuhr suggested that the very term "denomination" be defined on the basis of this pluralism. A denomination is a church that, at least for all practical purposes, has come to accept coexistence with other churches. This coexistence was brought about in America by unique historical circumstances, which were not intended by anyone and which at first were only accepted with great reluctance. Later on, a virtue was made out of the necessity, as religious tolerance became part and parcel of the national ideology as well as of the basic laws of the American republic. (Let me say in passing that I regard religious tolerance as a virtue indeed. It is all the more interesting to recognize that its original attainment was unintended. I incline to the view that most moral achievements in history have this character of serendipity. Or, if I may put it in Lutheran language, virtue comes from undeserved grace.)

Civil religion in America refers to a somewhat vaguer entity, an amalgam of beliefs and norms that are deemed to be fundamental to the American political order. In the last few years the idea of an American civil religion has been much discussed in terms proposed in an influential essay on the topic by Robert Bellah, but both the idea and the phrase antedate this essay.[2] Herberg, for instance, discussed very much the same idea using a slightly different terminology. The general assumption here is that the American

---

[2] Robert Bellah, "The Civil Religion in America," in Donald Cutler ed., *The Religious Situation: Nineteen Sixty-Eight* (Boston: Beacon Press, 1968).

3

polity not only bases itself on a set of commonly held values (this is true of any human society), but that these values add up to something that can plausibly be called a religion. The contents of this religion are some basic convictions about human destiny and human rights as expressed in American democratic institutions. Gunnar Myrdal, in his classic study of the Negro in America, aptly called all this "the American creed." The proposition that all men are created equal is a first article of this creed.

An obvious question concerns the relationship between these two religious entities. Different answers have been given to this question, and I can claim no particular competence in the historical scholarship necessary to adjudicate between them. Thus, to take an example of recent scholarly debate, I cannot say whether the civil religion of the American republic should be seen in an essential continuity with the Puritan concept of the convenant, or whether it should be understood as the result of a decisive rupture with Puritanism brought about by the Deist element among the Founding Fathers. Be this as it may, it is clear that the two religious entities have had profound relations with each other from the beginning. Nor is there any doubt that crucial ingredients of the civil religion derive directly from the Protestant mainstream of American church life, to the extent that to this day the civil religion carries an unmistakably Protestant flavor (a point always seen more clearly by non-Protestants than by Protestants, for people are always more likely to notice unfamiliar flavors). Thus, for instance, the codification of the rights of the individual conscience in the American political creed loudly betrays its Protestant roots, even when (perhaps especially when) it is couched in denominationally neutral language.

It is important to understand how the civil religion relates to the pluralism of denominations. Thus, in one sense, the civil religion is based on a principle of religious tolerance. Except for some isolated cases (Tom Paine was one), the spokesmen of the civil religion were not only friendly to the major churches but insisted that the latter were vital to the moral health of the nation. In another sense, however, the civil religion marks the *limits* of tolerance and indeed of pluralism. While it accepts a broad diversity of religious beliefs in the society, it limits diversity when it comes to *its own* beliefs. The lines between acceptable and unacceptable diversity have frequently shifted in the course of time, but to this day the category "un-American" points to the fact that there are clearly unacceptable deviations from the common civil creed. Belief in the divine right of kings, for example, was as clearly beyond the lines of official acceptability in an earlier period of American history as belief in redemption through socialist revolution came to be later on.

Unlike some of the democratic ideologies of Europe and Latin America, democracy in the United States was not inimical to the churches. The separation between church and state in the American Constitution did not, until very recently, imply that the state must be antiseptically clean of all religious qualities—only that the state must not give unfair advantage to one denomination over another. In other words, the assumptions underlying the separation of church and state were pluralist rather than secularist. It is no accident that there is no adequate American translation of the French term *laique,* and that (again, until very recently) there was no widespread demand that the American polity should become a "lay state" in the French sense. Indeed, a good case can be made that church/state relations in this country had the character of a "pluralistic establishment": officially accredited denominations were allowed to share equally in a variety of privileges bestowed by the state. Exemption from taxation and opportunity for chaplaincy in public institutions are cases in point. Just which groups were to be regarded as officially accredited, of course, was subject to redefinition.

To put it differently, the beneficiaries of the "pluralistic establishment" have been an expanding group ever since the system was inaugurated. First were added various less-than-respectable Protestant bodies (such as the Quakers), then Catholics and Jews, and finally groups completely outside what is commonly called the Judaeo-Christian tradition. The struggle of the Mormons to obtain "accreditation" marked an interesting case in this process. Recent court decisions on what (if my memory serves me correctly) were actually called "the religious rights of atheists," as well as recent litigation by Black Muslims, mark the degree of expansion of the system to date.

Historically, then, denominational religion and civil religion have not been antagonistic entities in America. Their relationship has rather been a symbiotic one. The denominations enjoyed a variety of benefits in a "pluralistic establishment," the existence of which was not only fostered by the state but solemnly legitimated by the civil religion to which the state adhered. Conversely, the civil religion drew specific contents and (in all likelihood) general credibility from the ongoing life of the denominations. Nevertheless, each entity has had a distinct history, with different forces impinging on the one or the other. Any assessment of the contemporary situation must allow for this distinction.

II

Keeping this distinction in mind, then, let us go back to the period around 1955: what was the situation at that time?

As far as denominational religion was concerned, the market was bullish indeed. These were the years of what was then called a "religious revival." All the statistical indicators of organized religion were pointing up. Church membership reached historically unprecedented heights. Most significant (or so it seemed then), it was younger people, especially young married couples, who became active in the churches in large numbers. The offspring of these people crowded the Sunday schools, creating a veritable boom in religious education. Church attendance was up, and so was financial giving to the churches. Much of this money was very profitably invested, and the denominational coffers were full as never before. Understandably enough, the denominational functionaries thought in terms of expansion. "Church extension" was the phrase constantly on their lips. There was an impressive boom in church building, especially in the new middle-class suburbs. The seminaries were filled with young men getting ready to swell the ranks of the clergy. Perhaps they were not "the brightest and the best" among their peers, but they were competent enough to fulfill the increasingly complex tasks required of the clerical profession in this situation. In the bustling suburban "church plants" (a very common term at the time) this clerical profession often meant a bewildering agglomeration of roles, adding to the traditional religious ones such new roles as that of business administrator, educational supervisor, family counselor and public relations expert.

The "religious revival" affected most of the denominations in the Protestant camp, and it affected Catholics and Jews as well. It seemed as if everyone were becoming active in his respective "religious preference." (By the way, an etymological study of this term derived from the consumer market would be worth making some day.) It was important, therefore, that all of this took place in a context of (apparently) solidifying ecumenism and interfaith amity. The Protestants within the mainline denominations were going through something of an ecumenical orgy. There were several church mergers, the most significant of these (long in preparation) being the union between the Congregationalists and the Evangelical and Reformed Church to become the United Church of Christ. The formation of this body in 1957 was widely heralded as a landmark in the movement toward Christian unity. Quite apart from these organizational mergers, there was a plethora of agencies concerned full time with interdenominational relations, ranging from the still quite young National Council of Churches to state and local councils. While some of these agencies engaged in theological discussion, most of their work was severely practical. An important task was the one formerly called "comity" and recently rebaptized as "church planning." Especially on the local level this meant that church expansion was based on research and on agreements among the denominations not to engage in irrational competition with each other—and particularly not to steal each other's prospective members. The religious market, in other words, was increasingly parcelled out between cartel-like planning bodies (and no antitrust laws stood in the way of these conspiracies to restrain free competition). Beyond all these formal processes of collaboration, there was a broad variety of informal acts of *rapprochement*—intercommunion, exchange of pulpits, interdenominational ministries in special areas, and so on.

It should be emphasized that most of this occurred within the mainstream denominations, which had a predominantly middle-class constituency. The more fundamentalist groups, with their lower-middle-class and working-class members, stood apart, undergoing at the same time quite dramatic growth of their own. It seems that the apartness of these groups was not much noticed and even less regretted by the ecumenists: the presence of the Greek Orthodox in the National Council was noted with pleasure, the absence of the Pentecostalists was of little concern. More noticed was the new relationship to Catholics and Jews. While the Roman Catholic Church still moved slowly in those pre-Vatican II days, there was little doubt that the old hostility between the two major Christian confessions was a matter of the past. And both Protestants and Catholics habitually expressed goodwill toward Judaism and the Jewish community, not only through such organizations as the National Conference of Christians and Jews but, more important, in local churches and synagogues throughout the country. Significantly, the major Protestant denominations increasingly took for granted that practicing Catholics and Jews were not fair game for evangelistic activity, thus at least informally including them in ecumenical "comity."

In retrospect it has come to seem plausible that at least some of this religious boom was deceptive. Even then there were quite a few individuals who questioned how religious the "religious revival" really was. Several factors contributing to it had very little to do with religious motives proper—high social mobility, with large numbers of people moving into the middle class and believing that the old nexus between bourgeois respectability and church membership still held; high geographical mobility, with migrants finding in the churches a convenient symbol of continuity in their lives; the postwar baby boom, with parents feeling rather vaguely that Sunday schools could provide some sort of moral instruction that they themselves felt incompetent to give (there are data showing that frequently it was the children who dragged their parents after them into the churches, rather than the other way around). As a result of these factors, there was a good deal of what might be called *invisible secularization*. In the midst of all this boisterous activity the deepening erosion of religious content in the churches was widely overlooked.

The "religious revival" in the denominations was paralleled by an equally impressive flowering of the civil religion. These, after all, were the Eisenhower years, aptly characterized by William Lee Miller, in a famous article in *The Reporter* magazine, as "Piety along the Potomac." Indeed, it was Eisenhower himself who made statements that could be taken as crystalline expressions of the mid-1950s version of the civil religion, such as this one: "Our government makes no sense unless it is founded in a deeply felt religious faith—and I don't care what it is." The political relevance of this faith, deeply felt and at the same time seemingly devoid of content, was expressed in another Eisenhower statement: "America is great because she is good." One may call this patriotic religion or religious patriotism. Either way, the content was America—its political and social institutions, its history, its moral values, and not least its mission in the world.

The rhetoric of the national government during these years was full of such religio-political formulations. Except for a small minority of anti-Eisenhower intellectuals, the country found this rhetoric quite in accord with its mood. Despite some shocks (notably the McCarthyite hysteria and the less-than-victorious ending of the Korean conflict), the mood was still one of national self-confidence if not complacency. There was still the afterglow, as it were, of America's great victory in World War II—a most credible conjunction of greatness and goodness. The postwar American empire was going well, with American soldiers mounting the battlements of freedom from Korea to Berlin. The Cold War, if anything, deepened the affirmation of the virtues of the American way of life as against the Communist adversary. (Not the least of the latter's evils was its ideology of "godless materialism.") The economy was going well, the dollar was king, and American businessmen as well as tourists circled the globe as emissaries from Eldorado. Indeed, many of its intellectuals were celebrating America (even if, as it later turned out, some of the celebration was subsidized by the CIA).

I do not want to exaggerate. I am not suggesting that there were no tensions, no doubts, in this mood. But compared to what happened later, this period impresses one in retrospect by the apparent unbrokenness—intactness—of the American creed. Just as the imperial cult of classical Rome was sustained by the unquestioned veneration of the familiar shrines in innumerable households, so the American civil religion drew its strength from the daily matter-of-course enactment of the virtues of the American way of life by innumerable individual citizens. I would not like to be misunderstood here: I am *not* saying that there was more morality in the 1950s than there is today; I *am* saying that such morality as was practiced was taken for granted in a different way. The American virtues, and the virtue of America as a society, were still upheld in the mind of the country as self-evident truths. I suppose that this assurance might well be characterized as innocence. To a remarkable degree, this rather grandiose self-image of Americans was reflected in the way they were viewed by foreigners— not least by the two major enemy nations of World War II.

If that was the situation in 1955, what has happened since?

To summarize the change, I shall take the liberty of making reference to my first book, a sociological critique of American Protestantism published in 1961.[3] In this book, when describing the notion that the world is essentially what it is supposed to be, I used the phrase "the okay world." I argued that religion in middle-class America served to maintain this sense of the world being "okay." I still think this was a fair description. The change since then can be conveniently summed up by saying that more and more people have come to the conclusion that their world is *not* "okay," and religion has lost much of its ability to persuade them that it is.

In denominational religion, the changes have differed greatly by class. The Protestant groups drawing most of their membership from *below* the upper-middle class have continued to grow, some of them in a dramatic way. They have largely remained untouched by the crises and self-doubts that have lacerated their higher-class brethren. Their theological fundamentalism has been modified here and there and their organizational style has been modernized, but as far as an outside observer can judge, their self-confidence as upholders of Evangelical truth has remained largely unbroken. The picture is quite different in the mainstream denominations.

---

[3] Peter Berger, *The Noise of Solemn Assemblies* (Garden City, N.Y.: Doubleday & Co., Inc., 1961) .

10

By the mid-1960s the "religious revival" was clearly over. All the statistical indicators started ebbing or even pointing down—membership, attendance, financial giving and (logically enough) church expansion. As budgets became leaner, the denominational and interdenominational organizations were forced to cut down on program as well as staff. Seminary enrollments stayed high, but there was widespread suspicion that the automatic exemption of seminary students from the draft had much to do with this (a suspicion that appears to be borne out in what is happening in the seminaries now). The market for denominational religion, in short, was becoming bearish. Not surprisingly, its amicable management through ecumenical cartels seemed less and less attractive. There appeared a marked reluctance to engage in further mergers, characterized by some observers (perhaps euphemistically) as "a resurgence of denominational spirit." The organizational mood became one of retrenchment.

More deeply, the 1960s were characterized in mainstream Protestantism by what can best be described in Gilbert Murray's phrase as a "failure of nerve." The best-known theological movements seemed to vie with each other in the eagerness with which they sought to divest the churches of their traditional contents and to replace these with a variety of secular gospels—existentialism, psychoanalysis, revolutionary liberation, or *avant-garde* sensitivity. The "death-of-God" theology was the grostesque climax of this theological self-disembowelment. At the same time the church functionaries, increasingly panicky about the fate of their organizations, tended to jump on whatever cultural or political bandwagon was proclaimed by the so-called opinion leaders as the latest revelation of the *Zeitgeist*. As was to be expected, all these efforts "to make the church more relevant to modern society" had the effect of aggravating rather than alleviating the religious recession. Those church members who still felt loyalty to the traditional content of their faith were bewildered if not repelled by all this, and those whose membership was motivated by secular considerations to begin with often felt that such commodities as "personal growth" or "raised consciousness" could be obtained just as well (and less expensively) outside the churches. The major consequence (unintended, needless to say) of Vatican II seems to have been to spread the aforementioned Protestant miseries through the Catholic community: the "failure of nerve" has become ecumenical too. At the same time, American Judaism and the American Jewish community in general have been driven by a variety of causes into a much more particularistic and defensive posture than was the case when Herberg announced the arrival of a "tripartite" American faith.

Just as there was good reason to doubt that the "religious revival" of the 1950s was caused by some sort of mass conversion, so it is unlikely that the subsequent decline is to be explained by sudden spiritual transformations. My own tendency is to think that secularization has been a long-lasting and fairly even process, and that nothing drastic happened to the American religious consciousness either after World War II or in the most recent decade. What happened, I think, is that the quite mundane social forces that made for the "religious revival" subsequently weakened. Most important, the linkage between middle-class status and church membership weakened (something that took place in England, by the way, in the wake of World War I). In consequence, the previously invisible secularization became much more visible. If you like, secularization came out of the closet. The inability of the churches to confront the emerging skeleton with a modicum of dignity almost certainly contributed to its devastating effect.

The changes that have taken place in the civil religion, I think, resulted partly from these changes in denominational religion (inevitable in view of the symbiotic relation between the two), and partly from extraneous developments in the society. To some degree, it can be said, the American polity has become more *laique* in recent years, and I suspect that this is largely due to the more openly acknowledged secularism of that portion of the college-educated upper middle class that finances what it considers good causes—in this instance, the cause of pushing secularist cases through the courts. The Supreme Court proscription of prayer in the public schools was the most spectacular of these cases. It was an exercise in extraordinary sociological blindness, though it appears that those who advocated it have learned absolutely nothing from the outcry that ensued. The same *laique* trend may be seen in the rigid resistance to any allocation of tax funds to church schools, in threats to the tax-exempt status of religious institutions, and in current discussion of various forms of chaplaincy. More important, a militant secularism today comes dangerously close to denying the right of the churches to attempt influencing public policy in accordance with religious morality. The abortion issue illustrates this most clearly. I doubt whether the tendency of the courts to go along with the secularists has profound reasons. Most likely it can be explained simply in terms of the parties attended by federal judges and the magazines read by their wives. (I assure you that I intend no disrespect to our judiciary—actually one of our more cheering institutions—but I am too much of a sociologist to believe that its decisions are made in some judicial heaven sublimely detached from the socio-cultural ambience of its members.)

There has thus come to be a threat to the old symbiosis between denominational and civil religion in America. And a more dramatic threat has come from much larger events in the society. It has often been said in the last few years that the legitimacy of the American political order faces the gravest crisis since the Civil War. Even after making proper allowance for the propensity of professional social critics to exaggerate, the diagnosis stands up under scrutiny. To be sure, there are important class and regional differences: what is perceived as doomsday by readers of the *New York Review of Books* may seem a less than overwhelming nuisance to the reader of a small-town newspaper in Kansas, and there is hard evidence to the effect that there continue to be large masses of people whose "okay world" has *not* been fundamentally shaken. Yet few people have remained untouched by the political and moral questioning induced by the headline events of the last decade —the continuing racial crisis, the seemingly endless fiasco of the imperial adventure in Indochina, the eruption of chaos on campus, and finally the shock of the Watergate revelations. I doubt if these events, singly or even in combination, are ultimate causes of the crisis of the American political creed: I think it is more plausible to see this crisis rooted in much more basic tensions and discontents of modern society, of "revolutionary" society, and to understand the events as *occasions* for the underlying difficulties to become manifest.

Obviously I cannot develop this point here. Suffice it to say that the survival in the twentieth century of a political order conceived in the eighteenth is not something about which I am sanguine (though, let me hasten to add, I fervently believe in the continuing effort to keep this eighteenth-century vision alive). Be this as it may, we have been passing through a process that sociologists rather ominously describe as *delegitimation*—that is, a weakening of the values and assumptions on which a political order is based. We have been lucky, I think, that this malaise of the political system has not so far been accompanied by severe dislocations in the economy: I can only express the hope that our luck continues to hold.

It may then be said that the civil religion has been affected by a double secularization. It has been affected by the secularizing processes in the proper sense of the word, the same processes that have come to the fore in the area of denominational religion. But it has also undergone a "secularization"—that is, a weakening in the plausibility of its own creed, quite apart from the relation of this creed to the several churches. Put simply, the phrase "under God," as lately introduced into the Oath of Allegiance, has become implausible to many people. But even without this phrase the propositions about America contained in the oath have come to sound hollow in many ears. *That* is the measure of our crisis.

IV

However prudent one may want to be with regard to the tricky business of prediction, it is almost inevitable in a consideration such as this to look toward the future. What are some plausible scenarios?

As we look at the future of denominational religion in America, a crucial consideration will be how one views the further course of secularization. In the last few years I have come to believe that many observers of the religious scene (I among them) have overestimated both the degree and the irreversibility of secularization. There are a number of indications, to paraphrase Mark Twain, that the news about the demise of religion has been exaggerated. Also, there are signs of a vigorous resurgence of religion in quarters where one would have least expected it (as, for instance, among the college-age children of the most orthodox secularists). All this need not mean that we are on the brink of a new Reformation (though I doubt if anyone thought they were on the brink of a Reformation at the beginning of the sixteenth century either), but it seems increasingly likely to me that there are limits to secularization. I am not saying this because of any philosophical or theological beliefs about the truth of the religious view of reality, although I myself believe in this truth. Rather, I am impressed by the intrinsic inability of secularized world views to answer the deeper questions of the human condition, questions of *whence*, *whether,* and *why*. These seem to be ineradicable and they are answered only in the most banal ways by the *ersatz* religions of secularism. Perhaps, finally, the reversibility of the process of secularization is probable because of the pervasive boredom of a world without gods.

This does not necessarily mean, however, that a return to religion would also mean a return to the churches. It is perfectly possible that future religious resurgences will create new institutional forms and that the existing institutions will be left behind as museum pieces of a bygone era. There are two propositions, though, of which I am fairly certain. First, any important religious movements in America will emerge out of the Judaeo-Christian tradition rather than from esoterica imported from the Orient. And second, the likelihood that such revitalizing movements remain within the existing churches will increase as the churches return to the traditional contents of their faith and give up self-defeating attempts to transform their traditions in accordance with the myth of "modern man."

The scenarios for the American civil religion hinge most obviously on one's prognoses for American society at large. Only the most foolhardy would pretend to certainty on this score. But one thing is reasonably certain: No political order can stand a long process of delegitimation such as the one we have been going through of late. There is only a limited number of possible outcomes to such a crisis of legitimacy. One, perhaps the most obvious one, is that the society will move into a period of general decline, marked both by intensifying disturbance within and a shrinkage of its power in the world outside. Not much imagination is required to see what such a decline would mean internationally. A second possible outcome is a termination of the crisis by force, by the imposition of the traditional virtues by the power of the state.

It hardly needs stressing that democracy and freedom, as we have known them, would not survive such an "Augustan age" in America. The third possibility is a revitalization of the American creed from within, a new effort to breathe the spirit of conviction into the fragile edifice of our political institutions. This possibility depends above all on political and intellectual leadership, of which there is little evidence at the moment. The future of the American experiment depends upon a quick end to this particular scarcity and upon the emergence of an altogether new unity of political will, moral conviction, and historical imagination—in order to preserve the society descending from our Revolution.

I have tried here to sketch a picture, not to preach a sermon. The social scientist, if he is true to his vocation, will try to see reality without reference to his own hopes or fears. Yet it must be clear that I do not view this particular scene as a visitor from outer space. On the contrary, I find myself deeply and painfully involved in it. As a sociologist I can, indeed must, look at the religious situation in terms of what a colleague has aptly called "methodological atheism." At the same time, I am a Christian, which means that I have a stake in the churches' overcoming their "failure of nerve" and regaining their authority in representing a message that I consider to be of ultimate importance for mankind. I suppose that a phrase like "methodological subversion" would fit the manner in which, again of necessity, the social scientist looks at political reality. With some mental discipline, then, I can try to describe contemporary America as if it were ancient Rome. But I cannot escape the fact that I am an American citizen and that the future of this society contains not only my own future but that of my children. Even more important, I happen to believe in the continuing viability of that eighteenth-century vision and in the promise implied by that oath—in my own case, first taken freely and of my own volition as an adult. Both for the religious believer and for the citizen, the assessment that I tried to make here translates itself into practical and political tasks. The elaboration of these tasks, however, would require a different format from the present one. In any case, it was not my assignment here.

16